Badger Religious Education

A course based on the QCA Scheme of Work for Religious Education for Key Stages 1 and 2

Key Stage 1

Teacher Book 1 with Copymasters
– for Reception

Christine Moorcroft

You may copy the activity sheets freely for use in your school.

The photocopiable activity sheet pages in this book are copyright, but copies may be made without fees or prior permission provided that these copies are used only by the institution which purchased the book. For copying in any other circumstances, prior written consent must be obtained from the publisher.

Introduction

Badger Religious Education helps teachers to put into practice the suggestions presented in the DfES/QCA schemes of work for the Foundation Stage and Key Stages 1 and 2.

The scheme recognises that teachers cannot be experts in every subject and have little time to prepare for the many subjects they have to teach. To help them to teach high-quality lessons it provides everything they need in order to prepare and teach each lesson (and suggests other materials which are easily available):

- lesson plans
- clear statements about what the children will learn
- lists of the resources required
- vocabulary
- background information for teachers
- introductory points for a whole-class or group discussion
- individual and group activities
- photocopiable activity sheets
- summary discussion points
- extension activities.

The posters and Pupil Books provide photographs of items which the children might not otherwise have the opportunity to see, such as places, buildings, works of art and artefacts, although their learning will be enriched if they also have the chance to experience some of these.

The scheme is divided into two sections which provide different types of materials to meet the needs of children of different ages:

Foundation Stage and Key Stage 1

The Foundation Stage and Key Stage 1 materials are:

- a set of 12 full-colour posters to support the three Units: Year R, Year 1 and Year 2
- three Teacher Books containing lesson plans and photocopiable activity sheets.

Key Stage 2

The Key Stage 2 pack materials are:

- four Pupil Books (for Years 3, 4, 5 and 6)
- four Teacher Books containing lesson plans and photocopiable activity sheets.

Contents

Harvest festivals

4-5	**Activity 1**	*Harvest time*
6-7	**Activity 2**	*Harvesting*
8-9	**Activity 3**	*Christian harvest festival*
10-11	**Activity 4**	*Harvest thanks*
12-13	**Activity 5**	*The sukkah*
14-15	**Activity 6**	*The story of Sukkot*
16-17	**Activity 7**	*Sharing, helping and giving*
18-19	**Factfile and resources**	

The friends of Jesus

20-21	**Activity 8**	*Making friends*
22-23	**Activity 9**	*Disciples*
24-25	**Activity 10**	*A circle of friends*
26-27	**Activity 11**	*Jesus, the friend of children*
28-29	**Activity 12**	*The story of Zacchaeus*
30-31	**Activity 13**	*Zacchaeus changes*
32-33	**Factfile and resources**	

Noah

34-35	**Activity 14**	*Noah's ark*
36-37	**Activity 15**	*God chooses Noah*
38-39	**Activity 16**	*The flood*
40-41	**Activity 17**	*The people we obey*
42-43	**Activity 18**	*The rainbow*
44-45	**Activity 19**	*Promises*
46-47	**Factfile and resources**	
48	**References**	

Harvest festivals

Activity 1 *Harvest time*

This activity focuses on the meaning of harvest and its place in the annual cycle.

Key words

cereal, crop, fruit, harvest, vegetable

Resources

- A shopping bag containing an apple, a pear, a packet of malted cereal, a packet of porridge and a packet of an instant oat cereal, a loaf of bread, a tin of baked beans, a packet of dried haricot beans, fresh and tinned carrots.

Focused discussion

- Show the children the carrier bag and tell them that you have brought in some of your shopping. Where do they think you did your shopping? Invite them to find out what you bought by taking an item out of the bag. Ask them to name each item. Write the words on the board in the form of a shopping list.
- With the children, read the shopping list. Do they know how the foods got to the shops, and from where? For the carrots, draw a flow-chart, working back from shop to farm.
- Ask the children which of the foods were grown on farms. Put them into a box. Are any left over? Where do the children think they came from? If necessary tell them about the sources of the processed foods.
- Introduce the word *harvest* for garnering crops, and the words *crop*, *fruit*, *vegetable* and *cereal*. Write the words on the board. Have the children ever harvested food? They might have picked soft fruits at a 'Pick your own' farm or blackberries in the countryside, or collected chestnuts in a city park. Introduce the idea of the hard work which people do (planting and caring for the crops) before there can be a harvest.

Using the photocopiable activity sheet

- With the children, read each word in the word-bank, asking them to point to the food from the carrier bag which matches it. Remind them about the food crops which have been changed since they were harvested (by cooking, mixing with other ingredients and being packed).
- Ensure that the children can recognise the word *harvest*.

- Ask them to match the words from the word-bank to the harvest pictures and to write the captions. They could read their captions to a partner to check.
- Encourage higher-achieving children to use information books to find pictures of food being harvested, draw the food harvest and write a caption. You could introduce other 'harvesting' words: *collecting*, *gathering* and *netting*.

Summary

- Invite the children to share their work.
- Ask them what they have learned about where fruit, vegetables and cereals come from, what happens during the harvest and what makes it a happy time.

Outcomes

- Most children will be able to talk about where cereal crops, fruit and vegetables come from. They will know that the harvest is when the crops are collected from where they grow, and be able to give examples.
- Some children will make less progress; with prompting they will be able to say that some foods come from plants, and name some of them. They will know that harvest means collecting foods from where they grow.
- Others will make greater progress. They will know that harvest means collecting foods from where they grow and might understand that all plant foods are harvested in some way. Using simple information books, they might be able to find out, and talk about, *how* some foods are harvested.

Extensions

- Discuss photographs of farms in different seasons, and when most crops are harvested in Britain. Explain how we can buy some foods all the year round and show the children crops from other countries whose seasons differ from those of Britain.
- Read *The Tiny Seed* (Eric Carle); make a pictorial flow-chart with captions to show the life of the seed. Encourage the children to share the wonder of a tiny seed growing into a plant. Talk about its struggle to survive, the seeds which did not sprout and the seedlings which died before they could grow flowers and seeds.

Harvest festivals

Activity 2 *Harvesting*

Here the focus is on the activities which take place during the harvesting of food. The children should first have completed the activity **Harvest time**.

Key words

catch, cut, dig, pick, plant, seed

Resources

- Some wheat, a pear, fish in a clear shrink-wrapped pack (or a picture of a commonly-eaten fish), a potato.
- Cards on which the names of the foods are written.
- Pictures of cereal crops, fruit, root vegetables and fish.

Focused discussion

- Show the children the foods and ask them to name them. Write the words on the board. Invite the children to come out and place the correct labels beside them.
- Remind the children of what they have learned about harvest time. Do they know where the foods come from? Ask them to sort them: 'Grown on plants'/'Not grown on plants'. Which is the odd one out?
- Mime the action of cutting wheat (as if with a scythe) and ask the children what you are doing to harvest the wheat. Tell them that modern farms have machinery to do this. Can the children remember the name of another cereal crop which is cut? Do they know any others? Mime the actions of picking pears, catching fish (using a rod and hauling in a net) and digging potatoes. Remind the children of similar crops about which they have learned.
- Discuss the children's experiences of growing plants, the sense of expectation after a seed has been planted (will it grow?), observations of the changes and how they feel when they manage to grow a plant until it flowers and then produces seeds.

Using the photocopiable activity sheet

- With the children, read the words in the boxes. Ask them to mime each action and name a harvest which they would pick, dig, cut or catch.
- Read the instructions on the activity sheet.
- Show the children how to draw a line from a word to a picture and copy the word. Ask them to do this for each picture and write the words in the boxes. Ask them to read their captions to a partner to check them.
- The children who complete the sentences in the extension activity might be able to draw, and write a caption for, another picture of a harvest activity.

Summary

- Invite the children to read aloud one of the words they wrote: another could mime the action and a third could name a food which is harvested in that way.
- Ask them how farmers or fishers might feel at the end of the harvest or fishing trip. Emphasise the hard work they have done, and introduce the idea of being thankful for the harvest.

Outcomes

- Most children will be able to name, mime and describe four different actions of harvesting, match the actions to the pictures and name a food harvested in each way. When prompted they will be able to talk about the feelings people might experience when they harvest a crop.
- Some children will make less progress; with prompting they will be able to name and mime some harvesting actions, and recognise that farmers are happy if they have a good harvest and unhappy if they do not.
- Others will make greater progress. They will be able to name, mime and describe at least four actions of harvesting, match the words to the pictures and name at least one food harvested in each way. They will be able to talk about the feelings people might experience when they harvest a crop, and relate these to their own experiences.

Extensions

- Explain that nowadays farmers can buy seed, but that in the past (and in developing countries) they had to keep some seed to plant for the next year's harvest. Plant some seeds from an apple or a tomato (both are easy to grow). Cereals such as wheat and barley can also be grown; this could be planned for the following spring. Clear a square metre of earth on which to grow wheat for harvesting each autumn; the children could even thresh, winnow and grind the grain (and make bread, with some supplementary flour).
- Introduce the idea that in some years harvests might be better than in others and that gales, floods and drought can destroy crops. This can be linked with the *Parable of the sower* (Mark 4: 3–9, Luke 8: 5–9).

Activity 2 *Harvesting*

Match the words to the pictures.
Write the words.

pick   dig   cut   catch

Write the words

We _____ wheat.   We _____ pears.

We _____ fish.   We _____ potatoes.

© Badger Publishing Ltd 2002

Harvest festivals

Activity 3 *Christian harvest festival*

The focus of this activity is on the ways in which Christians thank God for the harvest.

Key words

Christian, church, festival, God, harvest, hymn, pray, prayer, thank

Resources

- **Poster 1: A church at harvest time.**
- A tape-recording of a harvest hymn (**Factfile and resources**, page 18).
- Christian harvest prayers (**Factfile and resources**, page 18).

Focused discussion

- Do the children know what a festival is? Ask them about the special occasions they celebrate every year: for example, birthdays, Christmas, Holi and Id-ul-Fitr. Discuss how they are different from ordinary days – for remembering or celebrating something or for giving thanks.
- Read some Christian harvest prayers to the children. Explain any words they do not understand, and talk about what Christians say to God through the prayer.
- Listen to, or even sing, the hymn. Look for, and discuss, any words which are also in the prayers: for example, *creator, good, harvest, heart, thank*.

Using the poster

- Show the children **Poster 1: A church at harvest time** and ask them what kind of place it is and what they can see in it. Why are there fruit, vegetables, bread and other foods in the church? Who brought them?
- Explain that Christians thank God for the harvest each year by bringing food and flowers to the church. Point out the elaborate harvest loaves made specially for the harvest festival, and explain that only the best things are brought in. Tell the children that people also give money, which is used to help people in need.
- Talk about what Christians do in the church during the harvest festival; remind the children of the prayer and the hymn.

Using the photocopiable activity sheet

- Read the instructions with the children and help them to read the words grapes, bread and nuts.
- Show them how to follow a line, using a pencil, from the child to the gift, and how to write the word in the box.
- After they have completed the main activity, ask the children to draw and write what they would give to a harvest festival.

Summary

- Invite the children to show their work to the class. Are all their answers the same? Ask questions about the activity: for example, 'What did Ben give?'
- Ask them what they would give at the harvest festival, and why.

Outcomes

- Most children will know that Christians go to church to thank God for the harvest and that they give fruit, vegetables, other foods and money, sing hymns and pray. When asked, they will be able to say that harvest is celebrated every year.
- Some children will make less progress; they will know that a harvest festival is for saying 'Thank you' to God. When asked, they will be able to name something which Christians give at the harvest festival.
- Others will make greater progress. They will know that Christians go to church to thank God for the harvest and that they give fruit, vegetables, other foods and money, sing hymns and pray. They will be able to talk about something they would give, and why. They will be able to say that harvest is one of the festivals which Christians celebrate every year.

Extensions

- Discuss what happens to harvest gifts after the festival. Help the children to find out how local churches use them, and how they help people in need.
- If the school has a harvest festival the children could contribute to it and take part in the distribution of gifts afterwards.

Harvest festivals

Activity 4 *Harvest thanks*

This activity is about giving in order to express thanks.

Key words

gift, harvest, thank you

Resources

- A collection of *Thank you* cards

Focused discussion

- Show the children the *Thank you* cards. Read the words *Thank you* and ask why people send these cards. For what might they want to thank people?
- Talk about how it feels to be thanked and how the children feel towards anyone who thanks them.

Using the photocopiable activity sheet

- Read the instructions on the activity sheet and ask the children for what they can say *Thank you*.
- With the children, read the words *Thank you for...* on the activity sheet. Ask them to complete the sentences.
- The children should try to write their ideas without help; they could use the usual forms of support in the classroom, such as word-banks and picture dictionaries.
- In the extension activity the children could model their *Thank you* card on one of the cards they looked at earlier. Ask them how they would need to change it to make it into a harvest 'Thank you' card. To whom would they send it?

Summary

- Invite the children to take turns to read aloud a *Thank you* sentence. For what kinds of things did most of them say 'Thank you?' Ask them how they could make their 'Thank you' messages into prayers.
- Invite any children who have made a harvest *Thank you* card to talk to the class about what they have written and drawn and how the card is different from an ordinary *Thank you* card.

Outcomes

- Most children will understand that thanks can be given in writing and speaking as well as by giving. They will be able to talk about things for which they want to say *Thank you*.
- Some children will make less progress; they will understand what *Thank you* means. When asked, they will be able to give an example of something for which they have said 'Thank you'.
- Others will make greater progress. They will understand that thanks can be given in writing and speaking as well as by giving. They will be able to talk about things for which they want to say 'Thank you' and make a harvest *Thank you* card to thank God for food and other things.

Extensions

- Visit a church at harvest time; name the harvest offerings and talk about how they were harvested and from where. Let the children experience the atmosphere of the church at harvest time. Record or note down their comments on what they see, hear and feel. Find out about any harvest events, such as a 'harvest supper'. Back at school, talk about how the decorations are similar to, and different from, those on the poster. Tell the children that in different churches different foods might be brought in for the harvest festival because they are important to that place (for example, fish, cheese or local crops). Find out about the harvest in the school's locality.
- Make a collage of a harvest collection related to the school's locality. The children could write labels for the picture.

Harvest festivals

Activity 5 *The sukkah*

In this activity the focus is on the ways in which Jewish people celebrate Sukkot.

Key words

etrog, festival, fruit, Jew, Jewish, lulav, sukkah, Sukkot, vegetables

Resources

- Poster 2: In the sukkah

Focused discussion

- Tell the children that they are going to learn about Sukkot, a festival which Jews celebrate every year (in the autumn in Britain). Write *Sukkot* and *Jews* on the board.

- Ask the children if they have heard these words or know what they mean. Discuss their understanding of the words, telling them that Judaism is a very old religion and that at Sukkot Jews remember their history and give thanks to God.

Using the poster

- Show the children **Poster 2: In the sukkah** and ask what they can see in the big picture: point out the open roof, the branches, leaves, food and drink. Tell them that the people are in a sukkah, which they make every year for the festival.

- Discuss what the people are doing and what makes the meal special, and different from ordinary meals. Tell them that Jewish families eat in the sukkah during the festival (unless it rains); this helps them to remember God at this special time and thank him for everything they have. Any Jewish children in the class might be willing to talk about their experiences of Sukkot.

- Ask the children what else they can see on the poster. Invite them to describe the lulav and etrog (a citrus fruit), tell them the words *lulav* and *etrog*, point them out on the poster and let the children repeat them.

Using the photocopiable activity sheet

- Read the instructions and ask the children how they will decorate the sukkah. What will they draw on it?

- Read the question below the picture; ask the children what should be *inside* the sukkah.

- In the extension activity the children could use word-banks and picture dictionaries to find out how to spell the names of fruits and vegetables.

Summary

- Invite the children to talk about their pictures. Those who completed the extension activity could point to, and read aloud, the labels they wrote.

- Ask the children what they have learned about Sukkot. Emphasise that it is only at this special time that Jewish families eat their meals in a sukkah.

Outcomes

- Most children will know that Sukkot is a special time every year for Jews. They will be able to describe a sukkah and how it is used and, when asked, say that it reminds Jews to thank God for what they have.

- Some children will make less progress; they will know that Sukkot is a special time and be able to give a simple description of a sukkah: when asked, they will be able to say that Jewish people eat in it because it is a special time.

- Others will make greater progress. They will know that Sukkot is a special time each year for Jews, be able to describe, and label a picture of, a sukkah and say how it is used and that it reminds Jews to thank God for what they have. They might be able to describe *lulav* and *etrog* and to say that Jews use them at Sukkot.

Extensions

- Build a sukkah indoors or outdoors for the children to decorate with leaves, flowers, fruit and vegetables (and drawings of them and of a lulav and etrog) – *not to mimic the celebration of Sukkot,* but to experience the atmosphere of the sukkah.

- Visit a synagogue during Sukkot. Arrange for someone to show the children the sukkah and talk to them about it and about the lulav and etrog.

Activity 5 *A sukkah*

Decorate the sukkah.

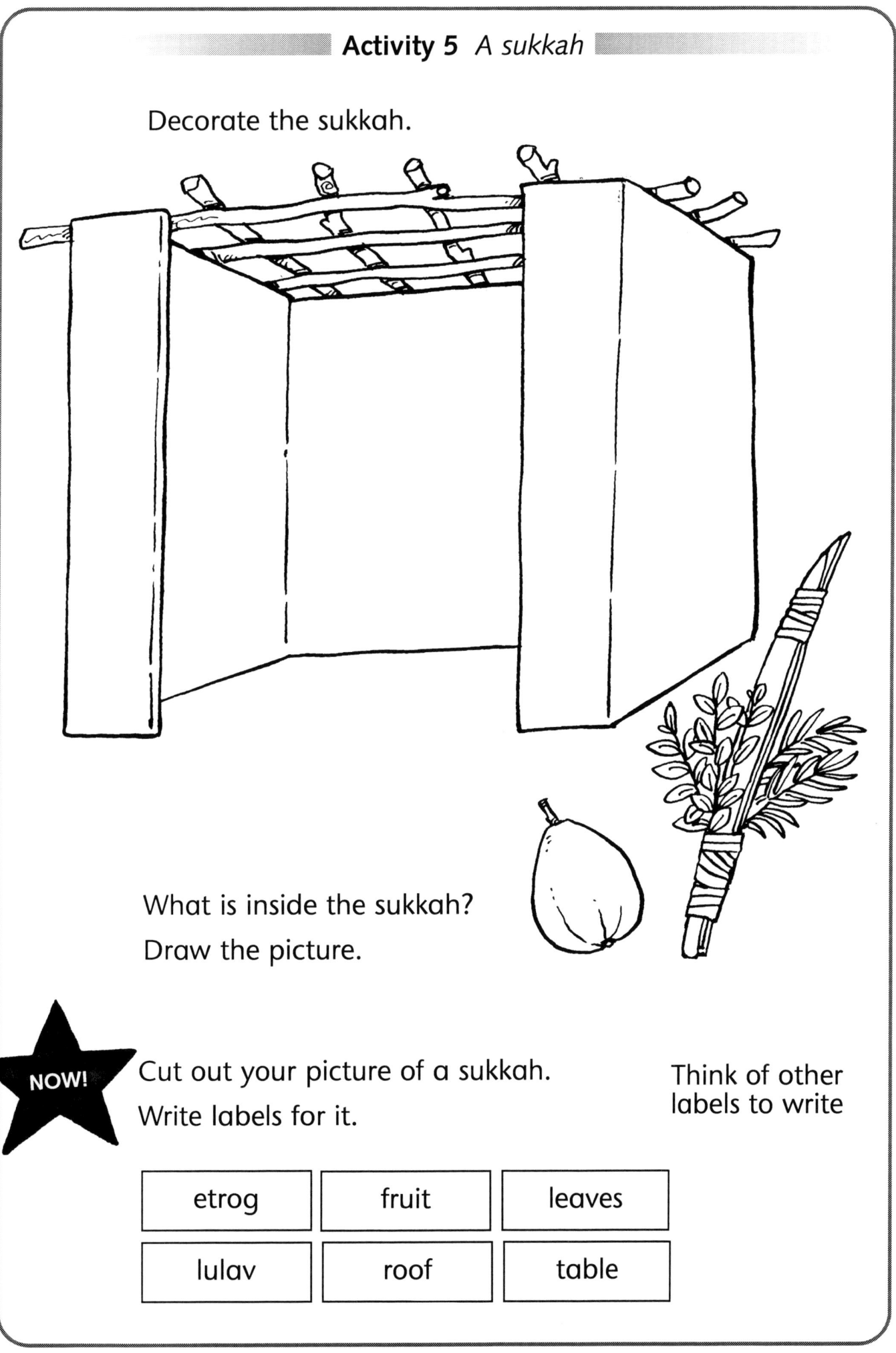

What is inside the sukkah?
Draw the picture.

NOW! Cut out your picture of a sukkah.
Write labels for it.

Think of other labels to write

| etrog | fruit | leaves |
| lulav | roof | table |

© Badger Publishing Ltd 2002

Harvest festivals

Activity 6 *The story of Sukkot*

In this activity the focus is on what Sukkot means to Jews.

Key words

celebrate, Jew, Jewish, remember, shelter, slave, sukkah, Sukkot

Resources

- A map of the world.
- **Poster 2: In the sukkah**
- Information about Sukkot (**Factfile and resources**, p19).
- The story of Sukkot (**Factfile and resources**, p19).

Focused discussion

- The children could talk about the dates of their birthdays, how often are birthdays, and why. What does a birthday celebrate? For how long does it last?
- Talk about familiar annual celebrations and festivals, and what is remembered or celebrated during them: for example, Christmas – the birth of Jesus; Divali – the return of Rama and Sita from the wilderness; Remembrance Day – soldiers who were killed in wars; and Id-ul-Fitr – the end of the fast of Ramadan. Talk about how long each celebration lasts (one day, many days or a month).
- Remind the children of what they have learned about Sukkot and tell them that it commemorates something from the Jewish scriptures. Tell them the story of the Exodus (The story of Sukkot, **Factfile and resources**, p19), and show them Israel, Egypt and the UK on the map. Explain the meaning of 'slave'.

Using the poster

- Show the children **Poster 2: In the sukkah**. Tell the children that the Bible says that God told the Jews that they were to live in shelters (sukkot) for seven days each year to remember how he looked after them in the desert. Explain that in some countries Jewish families sleep in the sukkah, but that in Britain it is often too wet and cold for that, so they just eat their meals there.
- Remind the children of the lulav and etrog; tell them that the Bible says that God told the Jews long ago that they should honour him with palm branches, the branches of leafy trees and citrus fruits (you could show them some citrus fruits such as lemon and lime).

Using the photocopiable activity sheet

- Invite the children to read the instructions aloud if they can. Talk about any new words in the story.
- Ask the children to talk to a partner about what they can see in the pictures and then to cut them out and put them in order.
- Encourage the children who undertake the extension activity to tell the story in their own words.

Summary

- Invite the children to read the story as they arranged it. The others check if it sounds right.
- Invite those who completed the extension activity to re-tell the story for the class, using the pictures as prompts.

Outcomes

- Most children will know that Sukkot is when Jews remember something from long ago and will be able to re-tell parts of the story. When asked, they will be able to say that God told the Jews that they must make shelters called sukkot (plural of sukkah) and give him their best fruits.
- Some children will make less progress; they will know that Jews build a sukkah each year to remember the shelters made by Jews long ago. When asked, they will be able to say that Jews say thank you to God at Sukkot.
- Others will make greater progress. They will know that Sukkot is when Jews remember those who escaped from Egypt long ago and made shelters in the desert. They will be able to re-tell the story and make links between it and the building of the sukkah and the offering of the best fruits of the harvest.

Extensions

- Show the children the parts of the Bible which tell of the Exodus of the Jews and the laws which God gave to them: Exodus 12–17 and Leviticus 23:40–42.
- The children could contribute to a class picture book with captions about the story of Sukkot. They could read the story to other classes.

Activity 6 *Jews long ago*

Cut out the pictures.
Put them in order.
Read the story.
Is it right?

They made shelters to sleep in.

They walked across the desert.

They ran away.

The Jews were slaves.

NOW! Cover the words.
Look at the pictures.
Tell the story to a friend.

© Badger Publishing Ltd 2002

Harvest festivals

Activity 7 *Sharing, helping and giving*

The purpose of this is to develop the children's awareness of how people can help others, and the emphasis on sharing and giving to others in Christianity and Judaism.

Key words

Christian, give, help, Jew, share

Resources

- Pictures of people giving presents, money, help and support.
- Poster 1: A church at harvest time.
- Poster 2: In the sukkah.

Focused discussion

- Discuss a picture of someone giving a present; ask the children why a present might be given. Their experience of presents might be mainly from birthdays and other celebrations. Ask them if they have given, or been given, something on an 'ordinary' day. Talk about what makes people want to give: for example, to show love or friendship.
- Show a picture of someone helping people in need and ask the children how this is different from the gifts they have just discussed and in what ways it is the same. Draw out the idea that when something is given it shows love or friendship (unless it is given in order to get something else).

Using the posters

- Show the children **Poster 1: A church at harvest time**. Remind them what they have learned about Christian harvest festivals and what happens to the harvest offerings afterwards. Find out what local churches do at harvest time to help people in need, and talk about sharing with people who have less. Point out that everyone has something to give; people can give their time: for example, to help with jobs, listen to someone who is worried or comfort someone who is upset.
- Show the children **Poster 2: In the sukkah**. Remind them what they have learned about Sukkot and how the sukkah is used. Tell them that Sukkot is a happy time when Jews invite people to their sukkah and share meals there. It is also a time when they share with people in need.

Using the photocopiable activity sheet

- Invite the children to read aloud the instructions and the words in the boxes.
- Ask them to talk to a partner about the pictures and about what they could give the people, and then to write the words in the boxes.
- Encourage the children who undertake the extension activity to think about someone they can help (a friend or someone in their family), and how.

Summary

- Enlarge the activity sheet; point to each picture and ask the children what they wrote, and why. Ask them how they feel when they help people and when someone helps them.
- Invite those who completed the extension activity to show the class their picture and to read aloud what they wrote.

Outcomes

- Most children will be able to name different ways of helping people, talk about giving presents and name something else they can give: for example, time, help, a hug or a smile. When asked, they will be able say how they feel when they give.
- Some children will make less progress; they will be able to talk about presents they have given or received, and say that giving presents makes people happy.
- Others will make greater progress. They will be able to name different ways of helping people and say that people feel good when they help, and are helped by, one another. They will be able to talk about giving and receiving love and friendship.

Extensions

- Children from faith backgrounds other than Christianity and Judaism might be willing to talk about how they give to, and share with, others: for example, *Zakah* in Islam (the requirement of making regular gifts of money to help others in need); the shared meals in the *langar* in Sikhism — taking turns to prepare and serve the meal for anyone who comes.
- Plan a sharing activity with the children deciding who needs help and how they can all contribute (for example, by selling their unwanted toys to help a charity).

Harvest festivals Factfile and resources

Activity 3 *Christian harvest festival*

A harvest hymn

> We plough the fields and scatter
> The good seed on the land,
> But it is fed and watered
> By God's almighty hand;
> He sends the snow in winter,
> The warmth to swell the grain,
> The breezes and the sunshine,
> And soft refreshing rain:
>
> *All good things around us*
> *Are sent from heaven above,*
> *Then thank the Lord, O thank the Lord,*
> *For all his love.*
>
> He only is the maker
> Of all things near and far,
> He paints the wayside flower,
> He lights the evening star.
> The winds and waves obey him,
> By him the birds are fed;
> Much more to us, his children,
> He gives our daily bread:
>
> *All good things around us...*
>
> We thank thee then, O Father,
> For all things bright and good;
> The seed-time and the harvest,
> Our life, our health, our food.
> No gifts have we to offer
> For all thy love imparts,
> But that which thou desirest,
> Our humble, thankful hearts.
>
> *All good things around us...*

Harvest prayers

> Holy God, creator, sustainer and renewer of life,
> grant that, secure in your goodness in the past,
> and rejoicing that you meet our needs in the present,
> we may work and pray for the coming of your future kingdom,
> that kingdom which is peace and prosperity, justice and joy;
> through Jesus Christ, who lived and died and was raised to life that all may share.
> Amen

From The Alternative Service Book

Leader: Creator and sustainer of all, at this harvest season we gather as your people to offer you our heartfelt thanks and praise.

Voice 1: We praise you for the bounty and variety of your creation
the succession of the seasons
the productiveness of the sod
the harvest of land and sea.
Creating and sustaining God.

Response
With wonder in our hearts, we thank you.

Circulated by The Arthur Rank Centre
http://www.countrysidematters.org.uk/farming/harvest-prayers.html

Activity 5 *The sukkah*

A sukkah should have three sides made of a natural material such as wood, with one side open. The roof must be of plant material such as pieces of wood or bamboo with gaps between them so that the stars can be seen and the rain can get in.

A lulav is made by binding together as a wand (at least 35 cm long), a fresh and perfect shoot of a young palm tree, a small branch each of willow and of myrtle. The etrog is a large yellow citrus fruit; a perfect fruit must be used. To symbolise that people love, serve and praise God, and read the Torah (the Jewish Law), they hold the lulav in the right hand and the etrog in the left, with hands close together, and wave them from side to side every morning of Sukkot (except Shabbat). The following prayer (translated from the Hebrew) accompanies the waving of the lulav:

Blessed are you, Adonai,
our God, ruler of the universe,
who makes us holy through your commandments
and has commanded us
concerning the waving of the lulav.

Blessed are you, Adonai,
our God, Ruler of the universe,
for giving us life,
for sustaining us,
and for enabling us to reach this season.

Traditional

Activity 6 *The story of Sukkot*

Sukkot (on 15 Tishri, which coincides with mid-September to early October) commemorates the shelters (sometimes called arbours, tents or booths) built by the Jews during their 40 years in the desert after they escaped from slavery in Egypt and followed Moses to find the Promised Land. (Exodus 12–17). During that time God set out many rules for Jews to observe, including the keeping of festivals:

From the fifteenth day of the seventh month, when the harvest has been gathered, you shall keep the Lord's pilgrim-feast for seven days. The first day is a sacred rest and so is the eighth day. On the first day you shall take the fruit of citrus-trees, palm fronds, and leafy branches, and willows from the riverside, and you shall rejoice before the Lord your God for seven days. You shall keep this as a pilgrim-feast... . You shall live in arbours for seven days, all who are native Israelites, so that your descendants may be reminded how I made the Israelites live in arbours when I brought them out of Egypt. I am the Lord your God.

New English Bible, Leviticus 23: 39–43.

The friends of Jesus

Activity 8 *Making friends*

The purpose of this is to develop the children's understanding of what makes a good friend and how to make new friends.

Key words

friend, make friends, friendly, new

Resources

- A story in which the characters are good friends (see **References**).

Focused discussion

- Read a story in which the characters are good friends. Ask the children if they think any of the characters in the story are good friends. How can they tell? List the friendly actions of the characters. Do the children know any other stories about good friends? Remind them of any book you have read with them and ask them what the characters did which showed they were good friends.

- Ask the children if they know any stories in which some of the characters were not good friends. You could remind them of any traditional tales they might have heard: for example, *The Three Billy Goats Gruff*, *Cinderella* or *Snow White and the Seven Dwarfs*. What did they do which was not friendly?

- Discuss what the children's own friends do which makes them feel good, and how they can help their friends to feel good.

- With the children, compile lists of what good friends do and do not do:

Good friends do ☺	Good friends do not ☹
share	say mean things
help	

Using the photocopiable activity sheet

- Ask the children what they would do or say if they wanted to make friends with someone. Write their responses on the board or on a large sheet of paper.

- With the children, read the heading and the instructions on the activity sheet.

- Ask them to write in the speech bubbles what Meg or Zul would say to make friends. What would the other answer, to be friendly?

- Encourage the children who undertake the extension activity to think about other ways of making friends. They should draw what they would do and write what they would say.

Summary

- Invite the children to read aloud what one of the characters in the picture might say. Ask the others to predict the reply, before asking the child to read out what he or she wrote.

- Invite those who completed the extension activity to show the class their picture and to read aloud what they wrote.

- Ask the children what they have learned about making friends.

Outcomes

- Most children will be able to name some of the things good friends do and do not do, and talk about how they can make friends.

- Some children will make less progress. They will be able to name something which good friends do and something they do not do, and give an example of what they could do or say to make friends with someone.

- Others will make greater progress. They will be able to talk about several things which good friends do and do not do, and talk, draw and write about what they can do and say to make friends.

Extensions

- Read other stories in which the characters show that they are good friends (see **References**) and ask the children to explain what makes them good friends.

- Make a class 'Friendship book' into which the children can glue their writing and pictures; it could include pictures for which they complete the caption *A good friend...*

- Invite the children to tell stories about how they made friends.

- Talk about how the children can help others who are shy to make friends. Talk about how the other child might feel.

The friends of Jesus

Activity 9 *Disciples*

The purpose of this is to introduce the Christian story of how Jesus formed a group of special followers and helpers called disciples.

Key words

Andrew, disciple, fishermen, friend, James, Jesus, John, Simon Peter, trust

Resources

- A Bible.
- The story of Jesus meeting the first four disciples (Matthew 4: 18–22, Mark 1: 16–20 and **Factfile and resources**).
- Cards on which are written the names of the twelve disciples: *Andrew, Bartholomew, James,* another *James, John, Judas, Matthew, Philip, Simon, Simon Peter, Thaddeus* and *Thomas.*

Focused discussion

- Show the children the Bible and tell them that it is an important book for Christians. Tell them that Jesus was a real person who lived long ago, that people long ago wrote about him and that we can read about him in the Bible.
- Read or tell the story of Jesus asking Andrew and Simon Peter, then James and John, to join him to be 'fishers of men'. Explain that he meant that they would go with him to spread the word of God to other people. Introduce the word *disciple* and write it on the board. Let the children repeat it.
- Ask the children how the fishermen might have felt when Jesus asked them to leave their work, and even their families and homes, to go with him. How would the children feel if they had to leave their families?
- Explain that the disciples, and Zebedee, the father of James and John, must have trusted Jesus. Also stress that they were grown-ups, and that the children must never go off with strangers, even if they think they can trust them.
- Invite four children to come out and hold the name labels *Andrew, Simon Peter, James* and *John*; read out the names of the other disciples who joined them later, asking children to come out and hold the labels. Tell them that Jesus gave the first Simon the name Peter, and that another Simon joined them later. With the children, count the 'disciples'. Read the names again. Does anyone in the class have one of those names? Do they know anyone else with a disciple's name?

Using the photocopiable activity sheet

- With the children, read the heading, the instructions and the word-bank.
- Ask them to write what Jesus said and the names of the first two disciples.
- The children who undertake the extension activity might need to be reminded of the story. Display the name labels *James* and *John*, and write another – *Zebedee*.

Summary

- Invite the children to read aloud what Jesus said. Ask them what the disciples might have answered. Invite those who completed the extension activity to show their picture and read aloud what they wrote.
- Ask them what they have learned about what people thought of Jesus.

Outcomes

- Most children will be able to re-tell the story of Jesus calling his first four disciples, and talk about how they might have felt on leaving their families, homes and work.
- Some children will make less progress; they will be able to say that Jesus asked some men to leave home and come with him.
- Others will make greater progress. They will be able to re-tell the story and talk about how the disciples (and Zebedee) responded to what Jesus asked, and how they might have felt at leaving their families, homes and work. They might remember the phrase *fishers of men* and be able to explain it.

Extensions

- Find out about the other eight disciples and make a frieze depicting all twelve, and showing the kind of work they used to do (if it is known).
- Help the children to enact the story of Jesus calling the first four disciples. The children could add words to express the feelings of the disciples (and their families) as they went with Jesus.

The friends of Jesus

Activity 10 *A circle of friends*

The purpose of this is to help the children to understand that people can make friends in many different places and that friendship is good for people.

Key words

choose, different, friend

Resources

- Pictures (for example, from magazines and newspapers) of people of different ages and races; people who look pleasant, unpleasant, friendly, aggressive, happy or miserable.

Focused discussion

- Show the children the pictures, one at a time, and ask them if they would like the person as a friend. Fix each picture on to a chart to record the choice of the majority of the children:

Discuss the children's choices: how did they decide which people they would like as friends? Did any of them make different choices? Ask them to explain their choice.

- What choices would Jesus have made? Tell the children that there are many stories in the Bible about Jesus befriending people who had no friends.

Using the photocopiable activity sheet

- Ask the children to name some of their friends at school. Do they have other friends who are not from the school? Ask them where they see these friends.

- With the children, read the heading and the instructions on the activity sheet.

- Ask them to draw their friends in the right places in the circle and write their names.

- Encourage the children who undertake the extension activity to think about grown-up friends of their families. Point out that they should not make friends with people their families do not know.

Summary

- Ask the children what they have learned about the friends they have.

- Talk about what people can learn about the way Jesus made friends with people. Write a summary of the discussion to display in the classroom.

Outcomes

- Most children will be able to name their friends and say where they see, or talk to, them. They will be able to say how they choose friends and know that Jesus made friends with all kinds of people, including those no one else wanted as a friend.

- Some children will make less progress; they will be able to name and draw some of their friends and, with help, say where they meet, or talk to, these friends. They will know that Jesus made friends with many people.

- Others will make greater progress. They will be able to name their friends from different places and say how they choose friends and how this differs from the way in which Jesus made friends with all kinds of people (including those no one else wanted as a friend).

Extensions

- Read stories about Jesus and his friends, including the story of Martha and Mary (Luke 10: 38–42, John 11:19–22).

- Make a display of paintings or photographs (taken by the children) of *Friends of our school* with sentences to which the children have contributed, saying why these people are friends of the school.

The friends of Jesus

Activity 11 *Jesus, the friend of children*

The focus of this activity is on Jesus as a friend of children.

Key words

> Bible, bless, children, disciple, friend, Jesus

Resources

- The story of the children being brought to Jesus (**Factfile and resources** and Matthew 19:13–15, Mark 10:13–16, Luke 18:15–17).

- The words of a children's Christian hymn about Jesus: for instance, *Jesus loves me!* or *Jesus is the Children's Saviour* (**Factfile and resources** and **References**).

Focused discussion

- Tell or read the story of the children being brought to Jesus. Ask why people wanted to bring their children to Jesus and why the disciples tried to stop them. Explain that people knew that Jesus was special and that Christians believe he is the son of God and that he can give God's blessing to people. Have any of the children had a blessing from a priest, minister or other religious leader? Ask them how they felt and what was special about it.

- Read the words of children's hymns and discuss what they say about Jesus. Ask the children what they think he was like.

- Talk about what Jesus said about children – "The kingdom of Heaven belongs to such as these" – and ask the children what he might have meant.

Using the photocopiable activity sheet

- Invite the children to read the instructions aloud if they can. Talk about any new words in the story.

- Ask the children to talk to a partner about what they can see in the pictures and then to cut them out and put them in order.

- Encourage the children who undertake the extension activity to tell the story in their own words.

Summary

- Ask the children if they liked the story, and why. What have they learned about Jesus from the story?

Outcomes

- Most children will know that children were special to Jesus. They will be able to re-tell the story of the people bringing their children to Jesus and might be able to say why they did this, why the disciples tried to stop them and why Jesus told them to let them come to him.

- Some children will make less progress; they will be able to say that children were special to Jesus. With help, they will be able to re-tell the story of the people bringing their children to Jesus.

- Others will make greater progress. They will know that Jesus was a friend to many people and that children were special to him. They will be able to re-tell the story of the people bringing their children to Jesus and to say why they did this, why the disciples tried to stop them and why Jesus told them to let them come to him. They will be able to talk about what Jesus meant when he said that the kingdom of Heaven belonged to people like children.

Extensions

- Talk about other people the children know who are friends to children: for example, those who work in and around the school, such as crossing patrol helpers. In what ways are they especially friendly to children?

- Link this with work in personal, social and health education on the dangers of making friends with strangers.

Activity 11 *Jesus, the friend of children*

Cut out the pictures.
Put them in order.
Read the story.

The disciples sent them away.

Then Jesus put his hands on their heads.

People came to Jesus with their children.

Jesus said, "Let them come."

Cover the words.
Tell the story.

© Badger Publishing Ltd 2002

The friends of Jesus

Activity 12 *The story of Zacchaeus*

This activity focuses on the good effects of friendship and how Jesus showed this when he befriended someone who was disliked by all his neighbours.

Key words

Bible, friend, Jesus, Zacchaeus

Resources

- The story of Zacchaeus (**Factfile and resources** and Luke 19: 1–10).

Focused discussion

- Tell or read the story of Zacchaeus the tax collector. Talk about what he was like. Ask the children if they think he had any friends and if he was happy.
- Can the children explain why Zacchaeus climbed a tree? Talk about occasions when they have been in a crowd, trying to see something, what they did and if anyone helped them. Did anyone in the crowd help Zacchaeus? Why not?
- Discuss what the people thought about Jesus making friends with Zacchaeus. How did Zacchaeus feel?

Using the photocopiable activity sheet

- Read the heading with the children. If they have completed earlier activities in this book they might be able to read the instructions for themselves. Talk about any new words in the story.
- Ask the children to talk to a partner about what they can see in the pictures and then to choose the correct word to write in the gap. They could read the story with their partner.
- Encourage the children who undertake the extension activity to draw and write what they know about the next part of the story.

Summary

- Invite the children to read their version of the story.
- Ask them if they can remember what happened next.
- Explain that the Bible does not say what happened after Zacchaeus promised to give away his riches and repay anyone from whom he had taken too much tax. How do they think Zacchaeus behaved towards others afterwards, and how might other people have treated him?
- Ask the children what they have learned about friendship from the story.

Outcomes

- Most children will be able to re-tell the story of Zacchaeus and will know that it comes from the Bible. They will be able to talk about what Zacchaeus was like, will know that people did not like him but that Jesus made friends with him
- Some children will make less progress; with help, they will be able to re-tell the story of Zacchaeus. They will be able to give a few simple facts about him: for example, he was rich, he was little and he climbed a tree to see Jesus.
- Others will make greater progress. They will be able to re-tell the story of Zacchaeus and will know that it comes from the Bible. They will be able to talk about what Zacchaeus was like, will know that people did not like him but that Jesus made friends with him and, through friendship, helped him to change his ways.

Extensions

- In groups, the children could enact the story. Allocate the parts of the characters (including people in the crowd); provide a collection of items for them to dress up in, and pictures of Biblical characters so that the children have an idea what they might have worn. The children (especially the 'crowd') could improvise the words. They could perform their play for the rest of the class or, in assembly, for the rest of the school.
- Discuss what people can do for someone who does not make friends easily. Invite the children to contribute to a set of instructions entitled *Be friendly.*

Activity 12 *The story of Zaccheus*

Write the missing words.
Read the story.

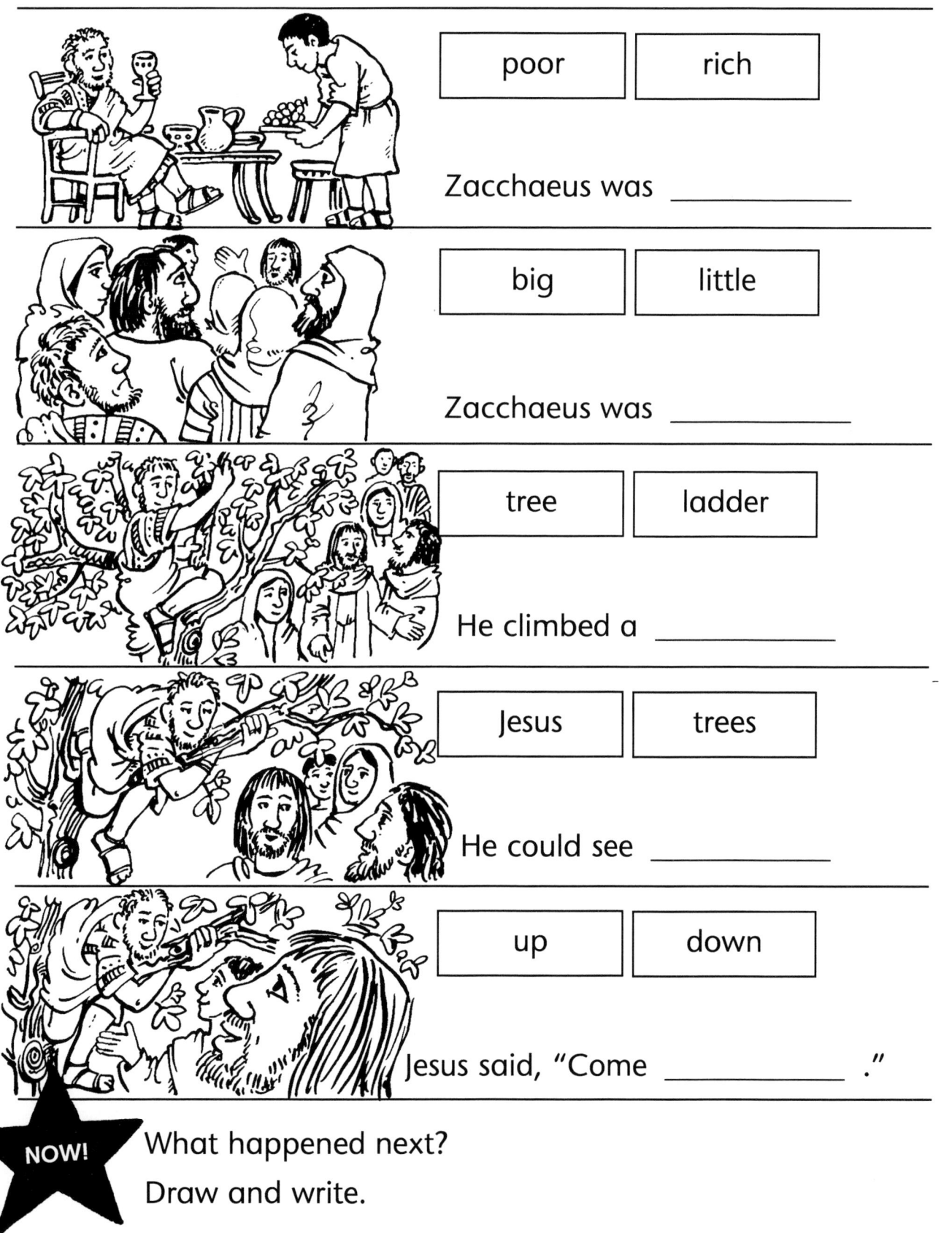

| poor | rich |

Zacchaeus was _____

| big | little |

Zacchaeus was _____

| tree | ladder |

He climbed a _____

| Jesus | trees |

He could see _____

| up | down |

Jesus said, "Come _____ ."

NOW! What happened next?
Draw and write.

© Badger Publishing Ltd 2002

The friends of Jesus

Activity 13 *Zacchaeus changes*

This activity focuses on how Jesus helped Zacchaeus to change his ways through friendship.

Key words

Bible, change, friend, give, Jesus, Zacchaeus

Resources

- The story of Zacchaeus (**Factfile and resources** and Luke 19: 1–10).

Focused discussion

- Remind the children of the story of Zacchaeus the tax collector, what he was like and whether or not he was happy. Why might he have been unhappy? What was important to Zacchaeus before he met Jesus?
- Ask the children how Zaccheus changed after Jesus went to his house. What was important to him afterwards? List their responses on the board or on a large sheet of paper.

Using the photocopiable activity sheet

- Read the heading and instructions with the children. Read the sub-heading of each picture.
- Ask the children how they will draw the face of Zacchaeus in the *before* picture. How will they show how he felt? What might Zacchaeus be doing? What else will they put in the picture to show what Zacchaeus was like?
- Ask them how they will draw the face of Zacchaeus in the *after* picture. How will it be different from the other picture? What might Zacchaeus be doing? What else will they put in the picture to show what Zacchaeus was like?
- Talk to the children who undertake the extension activity about the feelings Zaccheus might have had when Jesus picked him out of the crowd and how this changed his behaviour.

Summary

- Invite the children to read their version of the story.
- Ask them if they can remember what happened next.
- Explain that the Bible does not say what happened after Zacchaeus said he would give away his riches and repay anyone from whom he had taken too much tax. How do they think Zacchaeus behaved towards others afterwards, and how might other people have treated him?
- Ask the children what they have learned from the story about friendship.

Outcomes

- Most children will be able to draw Zacchaeus before and after he met Jesus, showing some of the changes: for example riches/no riches, unhappy/happy, without friends/with friends. They will be able to talk about these changes and write a few words about them.
- Some children will make less progress; with help, they will be able to draw Zacchaeus with his riches in the first picture and with a sad face. They will be able to indicate a difference between this and the second picture – drawing Zacchaeus without his riches and with a smile.
- Others will make greater progress. They will be able to draw, talk about and write captions for the pictures of Zacchaeus before and after he met Jesus, showing the changes: riches/no riches, unhappy/happy, without friends/with friends. They will be able to talk about these changes, write a few words about them and say what made Zacchaeus change.

Extensions

- Read stories about characters who change (see **References**). The children could draw *before* and *after* pictures of the giant, with captions. Talk about the changes in his feelings and in the ways in which other people treated him.
- Read stories in which unhappy or unkind characters do not change: for example, the wicked stepmother in *Snow White*, the troll in *The Three Billy Goats Gruff*, the wolf in *The Wolf and the Three Little Pigs*. With the children, change the story by making another character offer friendship to the mean character. Over the course of several days, re-write the story in a class book; the children could give it a new title.

Activity 13 *Zacchaeus changes*

Finish the pictures of Zacchaeus.
Write about Zacchaeus.

Before Jesus came

After Jesus came

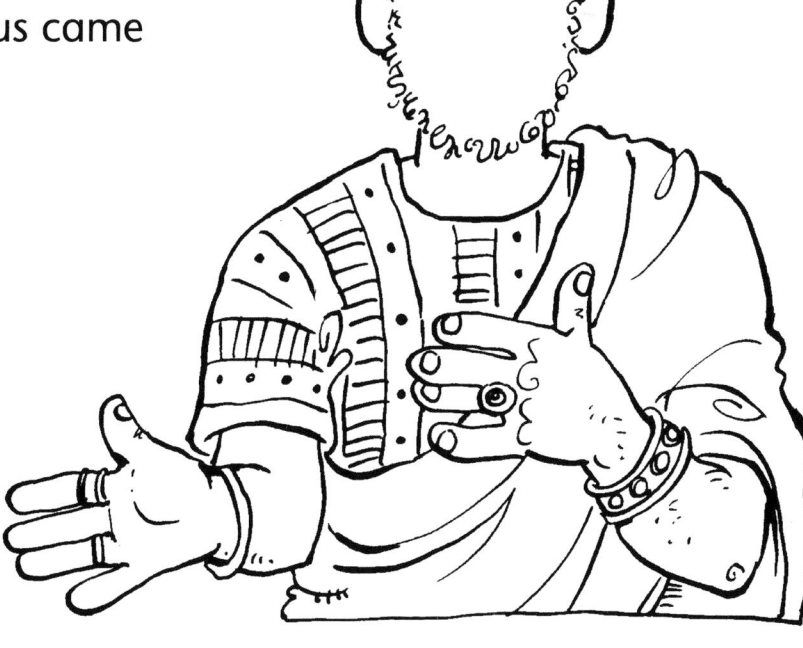

NOW! What made Zacchaeus change?
Draw and write.

© Badger Publishing Ltd 2002

Factfile and resources

Activity 9 *Disciples*

Jesus finds his first disciples

One day Jesus was walking by the Sea of Galilee. He saw two men fishing. They were casting their nets into the water. They were brothers called Simon and Andrew. Jesus said to them, "Come with me, and I will make you fishers of men."

The brothers left their nets and went with Jesus. He gave Simon the name Peter.

Farther along the shore Jesus saw three more fishermen. They were in a boat, mending their nets. There were two brothers, James and John, and their father Zebedee.

Jesus called James and John, and they left their boat immediately and went with Jesus.

Adapted from Matthew 4:18–22, Mark 1:16–20

Activity 11 *Jesus, the friend of children*

Jesus blesses the children

A crowd gathered around Jesus. Everyone listened in silence. They did not want to miss a word.

Some had children with them. When Jesus finished speaking, they moved towards him. They wanted Jesus to touch the children – to bless them.

The disciples saw this and rushed forward. They tried to hold the mothers and fathers and children back. Jesus went over to them. He said, "Let the little ones come to me. Do not try to stop them; for the kingdom of God belongs to such as these. People must come to the kingdom of God as a child does and then they can go in."

And Jesus put his hands on the children's heads, and blessed them.

Adapted from Matthew 19:13–15, Mark 10:13–16, Luke 18:15–17.

From the hymn *Jesus Loves Me!*

Jesus loves me! This I know,
For the Bible tells me so.
Little ones to him belong;
They are weak but he is strong.

Yes, Jesus loves me!
Yes, Jesus loves me!
Yes, Jesus loves me!
The Bible tells me so.

William Batchelder Brudbury, 1862
For the tune, go to
http://junior.apk.net/~bmames/hymnsjs.htm

From the hymn *Jesus is the Children's Saviour*

Bring the children all to Jesus,
For he is their dearest friend;
Having loved his precious jewels,
He will love them to the end.

Jesus is the children's saviour,
He has bought them with his blood;
Millions will be found in glory,
Singing round the throne of God;
Singing, singing,
Singing round the throne of God.

Civilla D. Martin

For the tune, go to
http://junior.apk.net/~bmames/hymnsjs.htm

Activity 12 *The story of Zacchaeus*

In Jericho a crowd began to gather along the road. Voices could be heard: "He's coming today!" Soon the road was packed with people. Then a little man wearing rich clothes and jewels came out of his house. He wondered what was going on. No one spoke to him. People became quiet as he passed. There were a few whispers: "Zacchaeus, the tax collector."

Then there was a commotion. They forgot about Zacchaeus. "Here he comes!" someone called. "Here's Jesus!"

Everyone pushed towards the road. Zacchaeus stood on tiptoe. He stretched his neck. He jumped. But he could not see over the people's heads.

No one made room for Zacchaeus. No one noticed as he climbed a tree and sat in the branches. "Now, hidden up here, I shall be able to see him," he thought.

When Jesus came along the road he looked straight up into the tree, and said, "Come down right away, Zacchaeus. I want to come to your house."

The crowd fell silent. Every eye was on the tree. Zacchaeus scrambled down and rushed over to Jesus. He took Jesus to his house and made him welcome. Outside, people stayed silent. Then some shook their heads and muttered to one another: "Jesus has gone to the house of a bad man."

They did not know what was happening inside.

Zacchaeus the tax-collector looked at Jesus, and said, "I am going to give away half of everything I have to help other people. If I have cheated people, I shall pay them back four times as much."

Jesus was pleased. "A great thing has happened in this house," he said. "You have found God. You have been saved from your wicked ways, Zacchaeus."

Noah

Activity 14 *Noah's ark*

This activity introduces a well-known story from the Old Testament of the Bible.

Key words

ark, Bible, flood, God, Noah, Old Testament

Resources

- **Poster 3: Noah.**
- Popular representations of the story of Noah's ark, such as a toy 'Noah's ark', wallpaper, fabrics and nursery print images of Noah, the ark and the animals.
- Picture books about Noah and the ark (see **References**).
- A Bible.
- Children's hymns about Noah (see **References**).

Focused discussion

- Show the children toys, fabrics and other everyday representations of Noah and the ark. Ask them if they know whom and what they are about. Do they know who Noah was and why the pictures show him with an ark and animals? What was an ark? The children might know that, in the story, Noah put two of every kind of animal in the ark, but do they know why?
- Read the words of a hymn about Noah, and ask the children what it tells them about him. Why do they think people remember Noah in songs and pictures?
- Show the children a Bible. Remind them that the Bible is a special book for Christians and Jews and that it is made up of two parts: the Old Testament and the New Testament. Ask them if they can remember any stories from the Bible.
- Tell the children that the story of Noah is a very old story from the Old Testament.

Using the poster

- Show the children the poster and ask them what they can see. Write the name *Noah* on the board, begin an animal word-bank on which to write the names of the animals the children can see. Can they think of the names of any other animals? Add them to the word-bank. Tell the children that two of every kind of animal went into the ark.
- Ask the children why they think Noah had to take two of every kind of animal into the ark. What do they think it would have been like on board the ark? How would Noah have had to organise the animals?

Using the photocopiable activity sheet

- Read and discuss the instructions with the children. What else will they draw in the picture? Ask them to think about the background, people and animals.
- Invite the children to suggest captions for the picture.
- Encourage those who undertake the extension activity to think about anything they know about Noah and the ark.

Summary

- Invite the children to talk about their pictures.
- Remind the children that the story of Noah comes from the special book for Christians and Jews; can they remember the name of the book? Can they remember from which part of it this story comes?
- Ask them if there is anything they want to know about Noah, his family and the ark. Make a note of the questions. Tell them that in another lesson you are going to read the story and that they can listen for the answers to their questions.

Outcomes

- Most children will know that the story of Noah is an old one from the Old Testament of the Bible. They will know that Noah built a big boat called an ark and that he took animals into it to save them from a flood.
- Some children will make less progress; with help; when asked, they will be able to say that Noah built a big boat called an ark, and that he took animals into it.
- Others will make greater progress. They will know that the story of Noah is an old one from the Old Testament of the Bible. They will know that Noah built a big boat called an ark and that he took two of every kind of animal into it to save them from a flood.

Extensions

- Make a large picture of the ark on to which the children can glue pictures of animals.
- Collect and display pictures of Noah and the ark and books telling the story. Encourage the children to read the books and look at the display by adding items from time to time, and talking about them.

Activity 14 *Noah's ark*

Finish the picture.

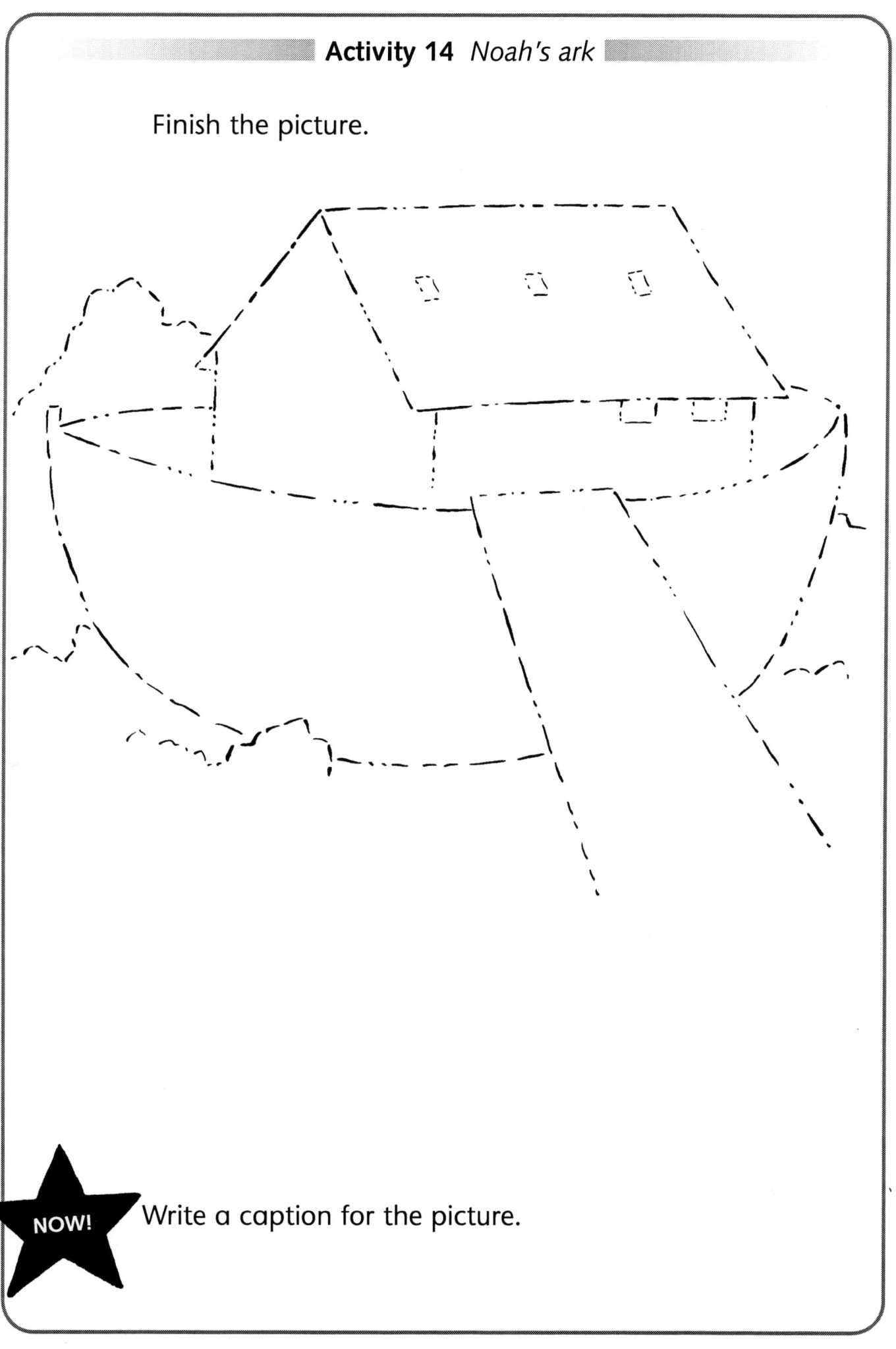

Write a caption for the picture.

© Badger Publishing Ltd 2002

Noah

Activity 15 *God chooses Noah*

This activity focuses on why God sent a flood, why he chose Noah to build the ark and the instructions Noah followed.

Key words

ark, bad, family, flood, God, good, Noah,

Resources

- **Poster 3: Noah.**
- A Bible.
- The story of Noah (Genesis 7 and **Factfile and resources**).
- The children's questions from the last lesson.

Using the poster

- Display the poster throughout the unit of work on Noah. Use it to remind the children of what they know of the story so far.

Focused discussion

- Using the poster, remind the children of what they have already learned about Noah and the ark, and that the story is from the Old Testament of the Bible. Show them a Bible.
- Ask them if they know why Noah built the ark. Tell them that you are going to read part of Noah's story to them. Display and read with the children the questions they asked during the last lesson. Read the first part of the story of Noah (to the point where he takes his family and all the animals on to the ark).
- Ask the children why God was going to send a flood. Why did he say he would save Noah? Talk about why Noah had to take two of every kind of animal.
- Discuss what it would have been like on the ark and how Noah would have looked after all the animals.

Using the photocopiable activity sheet

- Write on the board the key words: *ark, bad, family, flood, God, good* and *Noah*.
- Read the page heading with the children. If they have completed similar activities from this book they might be able to read the instructions.
- Read the sentences with them and remind them of the key words on the board.

- Encourage the children who undertake the extension activity to think about the next part of the story.

Summary

- Invite the children to read from their work.
- Ask them if they can remember what happened next in the story.
- Remind the children that the story comes from a special book; can they remember the name of the book? Can they remember from which part of it this story comes? (The Old Testament.)
- Ask the children about their experiences of floods, in real life or on television. Point out that when there is a flood it does not mean that anyone is being punished, but that the story was used to teach people long ago about how God wanted them to live.

Outcomes

- Most children will be able to talk about why, in the story, God sent a flood and why he saved Noah. They will know that it is an old story from the Old Testament of the Bible.
- Some children will make less progress; with help, they will know that Noah built an ark because there was going to be a flood. They will know that it is an old story from the Bible.
- Others will make greater progress. They will be able to talk about why, in the story, God sent a flood and why he saved Noah and to suggest reasons why Noah had to take two of every kind of animal on to the ark. They will know that it is an old story from the Old Testament of the Bible.

Extensions

- Begin a class book about the story of Noah, to which the children can contribute pictures and writing as they learn more about it.
- Ask the children to contribute to an illustrated 'animal' word-bank beginning with the sentence *On Noah's ark were*. From time to time, read the word-bank with the class and encourage them to add others to it.

Activity 15 *God chooses Noah*

Write the missing words.
Read the story.

| bad | good |

People were doing _____ things.

| bad | good |

Noah was a _____ man.

| flood | wind |

God said, "I shall send a _____ ."

| umbrella | ark |

"You must make an _____ ."

| family | house |

"Take your _____ on to the ark."

NOW! Draw the next picture.
Write what God said to Noah.

© Badger Publishing Ltd 2002

Noah

Activity 16 *The flood*

This activity focuses on the main events of the story of Noah. It encourages the children to empathise with the characters in the story.

Key words

ark, bird, flood, God, happy, hopeful, Noah, rain, rainbow

Resources

- A Bible.
- The story of Noah (Genesis 7 and **Factfile and resources**).

Using the poster

Display the poster throughout the unit of work on Noah. Use it to remind the children of what they know of the story so far.

Focused discussion

- Ask the children what they have learned about Noah. Invite them to re-tell the story so far. Tell them that you are going to read the rest of the story.
- Continue reading the story of Noah's ark. You could pause at the point where the ark stops on the mountain and ask the children what might be going through Noah's mind and what he might do.
- Talk about why Noah sent the first bird out from the ark, and what he learned; what did he learn when he sent out the second bird? Talk about how Noah's family might have felt at each point, focusing on when they might have felt afraid, happy or sad. Would they have been worried in case no one else had survived the flood, and they were alone in the world? Talk about what it might be like to be the only family left in the world.
- Have the children seen a rainbow? What did they feel? Did they want to keep on looking at it? Why? How might Noah and his family have felt when they saw the rainbow? Use the words *happy* and *hopeful*.

Using the photocopiable activity sheet

- Read the heading with the children.
- Give the children copies of the activity sheet. Tell them that the story has been mixed up. Read the caption of the picture *It rained for a long time*. Ask the children to find that picture. Read the caption *Then God stopped the rain*. Can the children find that picture? Continue reading the captions (in the correct chronological order) and asking the children to find the pictures.
- Give the children a piece of paper on which to glue the pictures in the correct order.

Summary

- Invite the children to read aloud from their picture story.
- Discuss what might happen to Noah and his family afterwards, the things which might worry or frighten them and what might happen to the animals once they were set free.

Outcomes

- Most children will be able to re-tell the story and talk about the feelings of the characters in the story at different points.
- Some children will make less progress; with help, they will be able to re-tell the main events of the story. They might be able to say when the characters would have been happy, sad or frightened.
- Others will make greater progress. They will be able to re-tell the story, and talk about the feelings of the characters in the story at different points and explain why Noah sent out the birds and what he found out by doing so.

Extensions

- Set up a role-play area in which groups of children could enact the story of Noah. Provide props such as large construction materials, clothing and 'animal' toys.
- Continue the 'animals' word-bank.

Activity 16 *The flood*

Cut out the pictures.
Put them in order.
Read the story.

The bird did not go.

The ark came to rest.

Then Noah sent out a bird.

It rained for a long time.

Noah sent out another bird.

Then God stopped the rain.

NOW! What happened next?
Draw and write.

© Badger Publishing Ltd 2002

Noah

Activity 17 *The people we obey*

The focus of this activity is on understanding the meanings of trust and obedience, and on what made Noah obey God and carry out his instructions exactly.

Key words

God, instructions, Noah, obedience, obey, trust, work

Resources

- Cards on which are written the words *obey* and *trust*.

Focused discussion

- Remind the children of the beginning of the story of Noah. Show them the word *obey*; read the word, invite the children to read it and ask them what it means. Ask them how Noah obeyed God. Remind them that the rain had not started when God told Noah to build the ark.

- What might Noah's neighbours have said when they saw him building the huge boat? Explain that Noah believed and trusted God. Show the children the word *trust* and invite them to read it with you.

- Tell the children that God told Noah exactly how to build the ark: how many doors and windows, how many rooms, how long to make it and what kind of wood to use. It was very hard work. Ask the children how Noah might have felt when he realised what a big job God had given him. He might have felt like giving up, but he kept on until he finished it: ask the children what made him do so.

Using the photocopiable activity sheet

- Ask the children to name people they obey: for example, adults in their families, teachers, lunchtime supervisors, headteacher, crossing patrol assistants, leaders of any clubs they attend and other people in charge of activities (for instance, swimming pool attendants). Discuss the people it is safe to obey – the people they can trust.

- Read the heading and instructions with the children and help them to read the captions to the pictures.

Summary

- Discuss the children's responses to the activity sheet. Emphasise that they obey people whom they trust.

- Whom do the children trust? How do they know when to trust people?

- Talk about times when the children do not want to obey the adults who are looking after them. Ask them for examples and talk about how they felt at the time.

- Return to the story of Noah. Why might it have been difficult for him to obey God? Point out how strange the instructions were – to build a giant boat and to take his entire family and all those animals on to it! Do the children ever think their parents or other adults ask them to do strange things? Can they give examples? What makes the instructions seem strange? Talk about things the children might have to do for which they do not know the reason.

Outcomes

- Most children will be able to talk about the people they obey and trust and to say why. When asked, they will be able to say that Noah obeyed God because he trusted him.

- Some children will make less progress. They will be able to answer questions about whether they obey or trust people like parents, teachers and strangers. They will know that God told Noah to build the ark and that Noah did as he was told.

- Others will make greater progress. They will be able to name people whom they obey and trust and to say why. When asked, they will be able to say that Noah obeyed God because he trusted him. They will be able to talk about the times when it is difficult to obey the people they should, and appreciate that Noah must have found it difficult to obey all God's instructions about building the ark.

Extensions

- Make a wall display entitled *The people we trust and obey*. Draw out the idea of obeying people because they want to help us or keep us safe. Link this to the story of Noah (God wanted to save Noah from the flood; he also wanted Noah to help him to save each type of animal, and he trusted Noah to carry out his work).

- Talk about class or school rules which should be obeyed, and why.

Noah

Activity 18 *The rainbow*

This activity focuses on the symbol of God's covenant with Noah and his descendants.

Key words

destroy, God, Noah, promise, rainbow

Resources

- Images of Noah (see **Activity 14**).
- **Poster 3 Noah**.
- A photograph (or drawing) of a rainbow.
- The story of Noah (**Factfile and resources**).

Focused discussion

- Show the children a picture of a rainbow. Do they know what it is? Write the word *rainbow* on the board. Ask the children if they have seen a rainbow, and what the weather was like. Draw out the idea that a rainbow appears when there is sunshine and some rain in the air (but not in heavy rain).
- Show the children **Poster 3 Noah** and other images of Noah. Can they find a rainbow in them? Why is it there?
- Re-read the end of the story and ask the children why God made the rainbow. What did he say about it to Noah?
- Discuss the meaning of the promise, and ask the children what they think it meant. Did it mean there would be no more rain? Or there would never be a flood anywhere again? Or that people would never be killed by anything in nature?
- Ask the children if they think it was fair that everyone except Noah's family died in the flood. What about the animals? Talk about other things which are not fair: for instance, some people are richer than others.
- Point out that some questions have no 'right' answer, but that people learn by thinking about them.

Using the photocopiable activity sheet

- Display a coloured picture of a rainbow. With the children, count the bands of the rainbow and name the colours in order.
- Give the children a copy of the activity sheet and again count the bands of the rainbow, asking them what colour each one should be. Ask them to put a coloured dot at the end of each band to help them to remember.
- Explain the word 'destroy', and ask the children what God destroyed through the flood.
- Invite the children to say what God promised Noah when he made the rainbow. Can they think of examples of some of the things he would not destroy? Ask them to draw and label one on each band of the rainbow.
- Encourage the children who undertake the extension activity to write God's promise in full.

Summary

- Invite the children to share their work with the class. Note the different things which they drew. Were they all living things? Talk about what might have been destroyed by the flood as well as animals.
- Ask the children what Christians and Jews might think of when they see a rainbow. What might the story tell them about how they should behave?

Outcomes

- Most children will be able to name some of the things destroyed in the flood. They will know that God sent a rainbow afterwards and that, for Christians and Jews, it was a symbol of his promise not to send another flood to destroy the world. They will begin to understand that there are some questions which have no 'right' answer.
- Some children will make less progress. They will be able to name some of the things destroyed in the flood. They will know that God sent a rainbow afterwards.
- Others will make greater progress. They will be able to name the kinds of things which were destroyed in the flood. They will know that God sent a rainbow afterwards and that, for Christians and Jews, it was a symbol of his promise not to send another flood to destroy the world. They will be able to ask questions about the meaning of the story and understand that many of them have no 'right' answer.

Extensions

- Continue the frieze of the story. Display the children's questions around the frieze. Display some of the answers they came up with, beginning *Maybe...* or *Perhaps...*
- Explore the meanings of everyday symbols. Display symbols such as a cross, a green traffic light, a red traffic light and a logo and ask the children what they think of when they see those symbols.

Activity 18 *The rainbow*

God promised not to destroy things again.
On the rainbow, draw the things God destroyed.
Write labels.

Write God's promise.

NOW!

© Badger Publishing Ltd 2002

Noah

Activity 19 *Promises*

This activity focuses on the meaning of promises.

Key words

keep, promise

Resources

- Display-sized copies of the Rainbow Guide promise and the Beaver Scout promise (**Factfile and resources**).

Focused discussion

- Remind the children of the story of Noah. What promise did God make? Was it a difficult promise to keep? Why?

- Are any of the children (or their older brothers and sisters) members of the Rainbow Guides or Beaver Scouts? Talk about the promises which children make when they join. Display and read the Rainbow Guide and Beaver Scout promises.

- Discuss each part of the promises in turn. What do the children think *to do my best* means? What would they do if they were doing their best? List examples. What would they do to be kind? List examples. What would they do to be helpful? List examples.

- Discuss the other part of the promise – *to serve God* or *to serve my God*. Talk about the different ways in which people worship God and do what they think he wants.

- Ask the children about promises which are hard to keep. How do they feel when someone keeps a promise, or when someone makes a promise to them but breaks it?

Using the photocopiable activity sheet

- Talk about promises the children think would be good to make. Write any key words on the board.

- Ask the children to talk to the others in their group about a promise their group could make.

- Give them copies of the activity sheet and ask them to think carefully about their group's promise before they draw or write. Tell them that you (or another adult helper) will talk to them about the promise before they write it.

- Ensure that you (or another adult) talk to each group about their promise. What will they have to do to keep it? Will it be too difficult to keep?

- Ask the children to draw and write their promise.

- Encourage those who undertake the extension activity to think up a symbol to remind everyone of the promise they have made.

Summary

- Invite each group to share its promise with the class. Write each promise on the board and re-read them with the children. Ask each group to tell the others what they will do to keep their promise.

- Talk about the outcome of keeping the promises. How will it affect everyone else? How can they help one another to remember, and to keep, their promises? They could use a symbol. They could also make a simple checklist to tick each time they do something to keep the promise: for example, *help someone*, *finish a piece of work*.

Outcomes

- Most children will understand what a promise is. When asked, they will be able to say what they will do in order to keep a promise and how some promises are difficult to keep.

- Some children will make less progress. They will be able to give an example of a promise and, when asked, give an example of what someone would have to do in order to keep it.

- Others will make greater progress. They will understand what a promise is. When asked, they will be able to talk about what they will do in order to keep a promise and how some promises are difficult to keep. They will be able to talk about the promise God made to Noah and some of them might be able to discuss how difficult it was to keep.

Extensions

- Discuss a class promise for the children (and adults) to make, and what everyone should do to keep it.

- Invite the children to design (by hand or using a drawing program) a symbol to remind everyone of the promise. Take a vote to choose one. Make an enlarged copy of it for display in the classroom.

Activity 19 *Promises*

I promise

 Draw a symbol to remind people of your promise.

Factfile and resources

The story of Noah

God looked down on the earth. He saw the people he had created doing evil things. Everywhere he looked there was evil. This made him sad and angry. He said, "I shall wipe these people off the face of the earth. I am sorry I ever made them."

And then God remembered a good man. The man's name was Noah. God said to Noah, "I am going to destroy everyone on earth. They are all wicked. I shall send a great flood to cover the earth. It will destroy every living thing."

Noah listened. God said, "I want you to make an ark. Make it like this: make a frame from wood; it must be three hundred cubits[1] long, fifty cubits wide and thirty cubits high; build three decks…" and God went on for a long time, telling Noah exactly how he must make the ark.

Noah took note of everything God said. He had never made anything like that before. He would have to do the work with great care. He sharpened his tools and began work right away.

Then God said, "Take your wife, your sons Shem, Ham and Japeth and all their children on the ark. Take two of every kind of animal with you – everything which crawls, creeps or flies. Take every kind of food for the people and the animals."

In seven days the ark was ready. Noah took all the animals and his family on it and closed the door and windows. The rain began.

It rained and rained.

It rained and rained for forty days. The earth was covered with water.

After a long time the rain grew lighter. Then Noah looked out of the ark. He held out his hand. It was dry! The rain had stopped.

Noah looked around. The ark was resting on a rock at the top of a mountain. Before long other mountain tops began to show. The flood was going down.

Noah wondered if the land was dry for them to go out of the ark. He opened the trap door and let out a bird. The bird flapped its wings and flew around. Then it came back to Noah. "Not yet," thought Noah. "We must wait a while."

After a few days Noah let out another bird. It flew away. Then it came back with something in its beak – a fresh green leaf.

Bit by bit the earth dried out. God said to Noah, "Come out. Bring everyone out. Bring all the animals out."

They went out. They looked at the sky. All the way across the sky there was a great rainbow: red, orange, yellow, green, blue, indigo, violet.

"This rainbow is the sign of my promise to you and to everyone who lives after you. I shall never again send a flood to wipe out all living things."

Adapted from Genesis 6–9

Noah

God looked down on a world filled with sin,
And said he'd destroy the whole earth with a flood.
But Noah found grace in the eyes of the Lord,
Who told him to build an ark of wood.
Build the ark! Build the ark!
They worked so hard from morning till dark.
Noah, Noah, did what God had told him to,
With Shem and Ham and Japheth too.
The work was done, though it took a long time.
Then God said, "There's still one more job you must do.
Bring all the animals into the ark,
Yes, bring them all in, two by two."
Fill the ark! Fill the ark!
They worked so hard from morning till dark.
Noah, Noah, did what God had told him to,
With Shem and Ham and Japheth too.
They entered the ark, and God closed the door.
Rain began to pour.
In the ark, in the ark,
As raindrops fell, and the sky grew dark.
Noah, Noah, in the ark is where he'll be
Safe with all his family.

© Copyright 1998 Steve Case

From the following website, on which the tune can also be found:

http://www.ukplus.co.uk/ukplus/clickcounter.jsp?id=404726&brand=Freeserve&search=hymns&pg=1&location=

---

[1] A cubit was not a completely standardised measure: it was the length of a man's forearm (about 50 cm). 300 cubits equals about 150 metres, 50 cubits about 25 metres and 30 cubits about 15 metres. You could mark out the length and width of the ark in the school grounds (if they are big enough) to show the children how big it was.

Activity 18

The Rainbow Guide promise

I will do my best to love my God
and to be kind
and helpful.

The Beaver Scout promise

I promise to do my best
to be kind and helpful
and to love God.

References

Harvest festivals

Children's books:
The Little Red Hen (traditional), Ladybird
The Tiny Seed, Eric Carle, 1987 (Puffin edition, 1997)

Books for teachers:
Photopack: Festivals, David Rose, Folens, 1994
Festivals Together, Sue Fitzjohn, Minda Weston & Judy Large, Hawthorn, 1993
See the websites for Christian hymns (below), for harvest hymns.

Sukkot:

Books for teachers:
Photopack: Festivals, David Rose, Folens, 1994
Festivals Together, Sue Fitzjohn, Minda Weston & Judy Large, Hawthorn, 1993
Religions of the World, Elizabeth Breuilly, Joanne O'Brien & Martin Palmer, Macdonald, 1997

Websites giving information about Sukkot:
http://uahc.org/ny/tinw/ReligiousLiving/ReligiousObjects/LulavEtrog.htm
http://www.myjewishbooks.com/what.htm
http://www.everythingjewish.com/Sukkot/sukkot_laws.htm
http://www.ou.org/chagim/sukkot/
http://www.jewfaq.org/holiday5.htm
http://www.torahtots.com/holidays/sukkot/sukkot.htm
http://www.holidays.net/sukkot/
http://www.us-israel.org/jsource/Judaism/holiday5.html

The friends of Jesus

Stories about good friends:
Leon and Bob, Simon James, Walker, 1997
Nini at Carnival, Errol Lloyd, Bodley Head, 1978 (Puffin edition, 1986
Handa's Surprise, Eileen Browne, Walker, 1994
Do You Want to be My Friend?, Eric Carle, Puffin, 1979
Letang's New Friend, Longman, 1994
Mr Nick's Knitting, Margaret Wild and Dee Huxley, Picture Knight, 1990
Little Bean's Friend, John Wallace, Collins, 1997

Websites for Christian hymns (with tunes):
http://junior.apk.net/~bmames/hymnsjs.htm
http://www.geocities.com/Athens/Troy/6082/
http://ingeb.org/spiritua.html
http://www.hymnsite.com/
http://members.tripod.com/~kcrowell/christian.htm
http://www.cyberhymnal.org/
http://www.newsongonline.org/midi-hymns.html
http://www.kt.rim.or.jp/~moclin/hymn-e.html

Stories about characters who change:
The Selfish Giant, Oscar Wilde, in *The Happy Prince and Other Tales*, 1888
The Bad-Tempered Ladybird, Eric Carle, Puffin, 1977

Noah

Children's books:
Noah's Ark, Lucy Cousins, Walker, 1993
Noah's Ark, Jane Ray, Orchard 1990
Professor Noah's Spaceship, Brian Wildsmith, OUP, 1980

© Copyright 1998 Steve Case

Badger Publishing Limited
26 Wedgwood Way, Pin Green Industrial Estate, Stevenage,
Hertfordshire SG1 4QF
Telephone: 01438 356907. Fax: 01438 747015.

Badger Religious Education – Key Stage 1
Teacher Book 1 with Copymasters – for Reception

First published 2002
ISBN 1 85880 890 1

Text © Christine Moorcroft 2002
Complete work © Badger Publishing Limited 2002

The right of Christine Moorcroft to be identified as author of this Work has been asserted by her in accordance with the Copyright, Designs and Patents Act 1988.

Cover picture: reproduced from *Noah's Ark* by Jane Ray by kind permission of Orchard Books. This picture is on Badger Poster 3 which is used in the units on Noah in this book.

Publisher: David Jamieson
Editor: Paul Martin
Design: Cathy May
Illustrations: Juliet Breese

You may copy the activity sheets freely for use in your school.

The photocopiable activity sheet pages in this book are copyright, but copies may be made without fees or prior permission provided that these copies are used only by the institution which purchased the book. For copying in any other circumstances, prior written consent must be obtained from the publisher.